F
PUDDING
RECIPES

*Traditional Ways to
a Man's Heart*

with illustrations by
Birket Foster RWS

SALMON

Index

Cover pictures: *front:* 'One of the family' by Frederick George Cotman RI
back: 'The way down the cliff' *title page:* 'Going home'

Printed and Published by J. Salmon Ltd., Sevenoaks, England ©

Pear and Ginger Upside-down Pudding

When turned out, this ginger sponge pudding is topped with pears and walnuts coated with butterscotch.

6 oz flour
1 teaspoon bicarbonate of soda
½ teaspoon salt
1 teaspoon ground ginger
1 teaspoon ground cinnamon
3 oz butter
4 oz soft brown sugar
4 oz black treacle

¼ pint milk
1 medium egg, beaten
TOPPING
2 oz butter
4 oz soft brown sugar
8-12 walnut halves
1 medium can pears in natural
  juice (approximately 4 pears)

Set oven to 350°F or Mark 4. Prepare the topping; cream together the butter and sugar and spread evenly over the base of an 8 inch diameter deep cake tin. Arrange the pear halves on top (cut side down) and place the walnuts attractively around them. Put the flour, bicarbonate of soda, salt, ginger and cinnamon into a large bowl. Heat together in a pan the butter, sugar and treacle until the butter has melted, but do not boil. Stir in the milk and egg. Beat the liquid ingredients into the flour until smooth and pour on to the pears. Bake for approximately 1 hour. Turn out and serve warm with whipped double cream. Serves 4 to 6.

Brown George Pudding

The Hanoverian King Georges were particularly fond of rich steamed or boiled puddings, hence the name of this pudding in which 'Brown' refers to its colour and not to the king.

4 oz fresh white breadcrumbs	**3 oz shredded suet**
1½ oz flour	**1 egg**
½ teaspoon bicarbonate of soda	**4 oz black treacle**
2½ to 3 oz soft brown sugar	**Milk**

In a bowl, mix together the breadcrumbs, flour and bicarbonate of soda and then stir in the sugar and suet. Beat the egg into the warmed treacle in a bowl and stir into the mixture with sufficient milk to make a soft, dropping consistency. Turn into a well buttered 2 pint pudding basin, covering the top with a piece of greased greaseproof paper and seal with kitchen foil. Steam for 2½-3 hours, topping up the water as necessary. Turn out the pudding on to a warm serving dish and serve with warmed treacle and cream or custard. Serves 4 to 6.

If preferred, golden syrup can be substituted for the black treacle, though this is not traditional and the resulting pudding will not be as brown.

Sussex Pond Pudding

A whole lemon enclosed in suet pastry makes this one of the classics of English steamed puddings.

PASTRY	**Milk and water to mix**
8 oz self-raising flour	**FILLING**
4 oz suet	**1 lemon**
2 oz fresh white breadcrumbs	**4 oz brown sugar**
Pinch of salt	**4 oz butter**

In a bowl, mix the dry ingredients for the pastry, using sufficient milk and water to form them into a soft dough. Reserve one third of the dough for the lid. Roll out the remainder into a circle on a lightly floured surface and line a greased 2 pint pudding basin. Leave some pastry overlapping the edge. Wash the lemon and prick it all over with a clean knitting needle, smear with the butter and roll in the sugar. Place in the lined basin together with any remaining sugar and butter. Roll out the remaining pastry into a circle. Use this to make a lid, sealing it with a little water. Cover with buttered greaseproof paper and seal with kitchen foil. Steam for 3-4 hours and serve from the basin. Serves 6.

Raisin Roly-Poly

A traditional boiled suet roll, beloved by men and best served with plenty of thick custard.

3 oz flour	**4 oz suet**
Pinch of salt	**12 oz raisins, stoned**
1 teaspoon baking powder	**1 dessertspoon sugar**

Mix the flour, salt and baking powder together in a bowl, then add the suet and sufficient cold water to form a soft dough. Turn out on to a lightly floured surface and roll into an oblong about ¼ inch thick. Sprinkle the raisins and the sugar on to the dough, then roll up like a Swiss Roll, damping the ends and pressing firmly together to seal. Sprinkle with a little flour, then wrap lightly in greaseproof paper and roll up in a lightly floured pudding cloth; tie the ends but leave room for the pudding to swell. Place in a saucepan of boiling water and boil for 3 hours, topping up the water as necessary. Serve cut into thick slices sprinkled with granulated sugar and accompanied by custard. Serves 4 to 6.

Moonshine

A very rich variation of bread and butter pudding.

2 oz butter	**¾ pint milk**
6 thin slices white bread	**¼ pint single cream**
(crusts removed)	**3 eggs, beaten**
2 oz sultanas	**Grated rind of half a lemon**
2 oz caster sugar	**Freshly ground nutmeg**

Set oven to 350°F or Mark 4. Use a little of the butter to grease a shallow ovenproof dish and use the rest to butter the bread generously. Cut the bread into strips and arrange in the dish, buttered side up, in layers sprinkled with sultanas and sugar, finishing with a layer of buttered bread. Heat the milk and cream to just below boiling point and stir into the eggs; add the lemon rind. Pour over the bread, sprinkle with nutmeg and leave to stand for 20 minutes. Bake for 30-40 minutes until the custard is set and the top is crisp and golden. Serves 4.

Prince Albert's Pudding

A great many dishes, sweet and savoury, have been named after members of the Royal Family, among them this popular Victorian pudding that contains raisins and candied peel and is flavoured with mace.

4 oz sugar	**Pinch of salt**
4 oz butter, softened	**6 oz raisins**
2 eggs, beaten	**1 oz candied peel, finely chopped**
4 oz flour	**½ teaspoon ground mace**
¼ teaspoon baking powder	**A little milk, if necessary**

In a bowl, cream the sugar and butter together until light and fluffy, then beat in the eggs. Sift together the flour, baking powder and salt and fold into the egg mixture, then add the raisins, peel and mace, adding a little milk if the mixture seems too stiff. Spoon the mixture into a well buttered 2 pint pudding basin, cover with lightly buttered greaseproof paper and seal with kitchen foil. Steam for 1½-2 hours, topping up the water as necessary. Turn out on to a warmed serving dish and serve with pouring cream or custard. Serves 4 to 6.

Fig Pudding

A rich and fruity sponge pudding flavoured with brandy, rum or fortified wine.

8 oz dried figs	**1 oz ground almonds**
2 oz raisins	**Pinch of mixed spice**
3 oz butter	**Grated rind of ½ a lemon**
3 oz soft brown sugar	**1 egg**
3 oz flour	**2 to 3 tablespoons brandy,**
2 oz fresh white breadcrumbs	**rum, Madeira or sherry**

Soak the figs and raisins overnight in cold weak tea, to which a little lemon juice has been added. Next morning, drain the fruit well and chop the figs finely. In a bowl, cream the butter and sugar together, then fold in the flour a little at a time. Add the breadcrumbs, ground almonds, spice, lemon rind, figs and raisins and combine well. Beat the egg with the brandy, rum, Madeira or sherry and add to the mixture. Stir well, turn into a 1½ to 2 pint buttered pudding basin and cover with buttered greaseproof paper and seal with kitchen foil. Cover and steam for 3½-4 hours, topping up the water as necessary, until the pudding is springy and well risen. Turn out on to a warm plate and serve with custard or cream. Serves 4 to 6.

Special Bread Pudding

A delicious, old-fashioned pudding made with butter rather than suet.

8 oz stale bread	**½ teaspoon ground mixed spice**
½ pt milk	**4 oz butter, melted**
4 oz currants or sultanas	**1 egg**
3 oz sugar	**Caster sugar for topping**

Cut away any hard crusts from the bread, break it into pieces and put into the milk to soak for about ½ to 1 hour. Set oven to 350°F or Mark 4 and grease a 2-2½ pint ovenproof dish. Squeeze out the excess milk from the bread, put it into a bowl and break up any lumps with a wooden spoon. Put all the other ingredients into the bowl with the bread and mix very well, adding a little milk, if necessary, to produce a soft, dropping consistency. Put the mixture into the baking dish, spread out and bake for about 1 hour until golden. Remove from the oven and sprinkle over with caster sugar. Serve hot with custard or cold, sliced for tea. Serves 4 to 6.

Pumpkin Pie

An Autumn pudding containing pumpkin, apple and dried fruit.

1 lb ripe pumpkin, diced
½ lb apple, diced
½ lb currants
½ lb sultanas
4 oz brown sugar

1 teaspoon mixed spice
1 teaspoon ground ginger
Juice of a lemon
¾ lb shortcrust pastry
Egg white for brushing

Sugar for sprinkling

Set oven to 400°F or Mark 6. Mix together in a bowl all the ingredients and put the mixture into a large pie dish; oval or round about 9 inches in diameter and 1½-2 inches deep. Roll out the pastry on a lightly floured surface and cover the pumpkin mixture. Trim and decorate, brush with egg white and sprinkle with sugar. Put in the oven and bake for 20 minutes. Then reduce the temperature to 350°F or Mark 4 and bake for a further 20 minutes, or until the pastry is golden brown. Serves 6.

Glastonbury Pudding

A delicious sponge pudding layered with apricots, apples and apricot jam, from Somerset.

SPONGE
4 oz butter
4 oz caster sugar
2 medium eggs
6 oz wholemeal self-raising flour
Rind of half a lemon,
  finely grated

FILLING
1 medium cooking apple, peeled,
  cored and coarsely grated
3 oz 'No-soak' dried apricots,
  finely chopped
3 tablespoons apricot jam
Juice of half a lemon

Grease a 1½ pint pudding basin. Prepare the sponge mixture either by the traditional creaming method and flavouring with the lemon rind or by putting all the ingredients into a food processor and mixing for 30 seconds. Mix together all the filling ingredients. Place a layer of sponge mixture into the base of the pudding basin and top with some of the filling. Continue alternating the layers and finish with a layer of sponge mixture. Cover with a circle of greaseproof paper and then cover and seal with kitchen foil. Steam for 2 hours. Remove covering and leave the pudding in the basin for 5 minutes before turning out on to a warm serving dish. Serve hot with custard or cream. Serves 4 to 6.

Blackberry Roll

A baked fruit roll containing apples and blackberries spiced with cinnamon.

8 oz blackberries, hulled and washed
1 medium cooking apple, peeled,
  cored and finely chopped
3 oz raisins
6 oz sugar
1 teaspoon ground cinnamon

1 teaspoon lemon juice
2 tablespoons water
A 'walnut' of butter
2 oz flaked almonds
8 oz shortcrust pastry
Beaten egg or milk to glaze

Place the fruit, sugar, cinnamon, lemon juice, water and butter in a saucepan and simmer, stirring frequently, until the mixture has thickened to a marmalade-like consistency. Cool, then stir in the almonds. Set oven to 400°F or Mark 6. Roll out the pastry on a lightly floured surface to form a neat rectangle and brush *very* lightly with beaten egg or milk. Allow to dry, then spread the fruit mixture over to within approximately half an inch of the edges of the pastry. Roll up carefully, like a Swiss Roll, seal the edges well with water, then brush with beaten egg or milk to glaze. Place on a lightly greased baking sheet and bake for 25-30 minutes or until golden brown. Serve, sliced with cream or custard. Serves 4.

'Rural bliss'

Ipswich Almond Pudding

This light, almond flavoured Suffolk pudding contains cream, eggs and orange flower water.

¾ **pint milk**
5 fluid oz double cream
2 oz fresh white breadcrumbs,
   finely grated
3 oz sugar

6 oz ground almonds
1 teaspoon orange flower water
   or rose water
3 eggs, beaten
1 oz butter

Set oven to 350°F or Mark 4. Warm the milk and cream together in a saucepan. Put the breadcrumbs into a bowl, then add the milk/cream mixture and leave to stand for 5 minutes. Add the sugar, ground almonds and orange water or rose water and leave to stand for a further 10 minutes until all the liquid has been absorbed. Stir in the eggs, blending well. Pour the mixture into a buttered 2 pint pie dish. Dot the surface with the butter. Set the pie dish in a roasting tin. Pour boiling water into the tin until it comes about a quarter of the way up the side of the pie dish. Bake for 30 minutes. Serve accompanied by single cream. Serves 4.

Greengage Tart

In the 18th century, Sir William Gage planted some unknown plum trees in the orchard of his estate near Bury St. Edmunds in Suffolk. They produced delicious yellow-green fruit, that became known as Green Gage's Plums, later corrupted to Greengage.

8 oz shortcrust pastry
1 lb greengages, washed, halved and stoned

1 dessertspoon sugar, optional
2 eggs, beaten
1 pint single cream

Set oven to 400°F or Mark 6. Grease a 7 inch flan dish. Roll out the pastry on a lightly floured surface, line the dish, trim and bake blind for 10 minutes. Arrange the greengages, cut side down, in the pastry case, and sprinkle with the sugar, if desired. Beat the eggs and cream together and strain over the greengages. Cook for 30-35 minutes or until the filling is golden and puffed up. Serve warm with extra cream, if desired. Serves 4.

Harvest Pudding

A variation of bread and butter pudding, with an apple, suet and raisin filling.

6-8 slices of buttered bread, medium-sliced	**3 oz soft brown sugar**
	2 oz raisins
1 lb cooking apples, peeled, cored and sliced	**Grated rind of one lemon**
	2 medium eggs
2 oz shredded suet	**½ pint milk**

Line a pie dish with some of the buttered bread. Mix together the apples, suet, sugar, raisins and lemon rind. Fill the pie dish with the mixture and cover with more buttered bread (buttered side uppermost). Beat together the eggs and milk and pour over the top of the bread. Cover and leave to stand in a cool place for approximately 2 hours. Bake in a pre-heated oven at 350°F or Mark 4 for approximately 1 hour. Serve warm with clotted cream. Serves 4 to 6.

Kentish Pan Cake

Apple pancakes, fried and stacked as a cake and served cut into wedges.

3 eggs	4 oz flour
2 whites of egg	A pinch of powdered ginger
¼ pink milk	A pinch of salt
¼ pint double cream	Grated nutmeg to taste
2 tablespoons sherry	1 tablespoon caster sugar
3 dessertspoons brandy	½ medium sized cooking apple

Lard for frying

Put the eggs and the extra egg whites, milk, cream, sherry, brandy, flour, salt and the spices in a mixing bowl. Beat well until smooth. Peel and core the apple and chop it finely. Add the sugar and apple to the batter and leave to stand in a cool place for 30 minutes. Lightly grease the frying pan with the lard, fry the pancakes and stack them on a large piece of greaseproof paper. When completed, wrap them in the paper and keep warm until needed. Then turn the 'stack' on to a warm plate and dredge with icing sugar. Cut into wedges and serve with whipped cream and puréed apple. Serves 6.

Belvoir House Pudding

A delicious steamed sponge pudding flavoured with sherry from the Leicestershire home of the Dukes of Rutland.

4 oz butter	**2 oz glacé cherries, chopped**
4 oz caster sugar	**½ oz angelica, chopped**
2 eggs, beaten	**1 tablespoon coffee essence**
4 oz flour	**or 2 tablespoons cold**
½ teaspoon baking powder	**black coffee**
Pinch of salt	**2 tablespoons rum or sherry**

Set oven to 350°F or Mark 4. In a bowl, cream the butter until soft, then add the sugar, mixing until light and fluffy. Beat in the eggs, a little at a time. Sift the flour, baking powder and salt together, and fold into the mixture. Mix the cherries and angelica together and stir in, with the coffee essence or black coffee and the rum or sherry. Turn into a well greased 1½-2 pint ovenproof dish or a fluted cake tin and bake for 35-40 minutes until well risen and springy, covering the top with a piece of kitchen foil if it appears to be browning too quickly. Turn out on to a warm serving dish and serve with rum or sherry flavoured whipped cream or custard. Serves 4.

Treacle and Marmalade Tart

A variation of the usual treacle tart recipe, with the addition of marmalade to the filling.

8 oz shortcrust pastry   **4 oz marmalade**
8 oz golden syrup   **8 oz white breadcrumbs**
2 tablespoons lemon juice

Set oven to 350°F or Mark 4. Roll out the pastry on a lightly floured surface and line an 8 inch flan dish. Trim the edges and reserve the extra pastry. Sprinkle the breadcrumbs evenly over the pastry base. Warm the syrup and marmalade very gently in a saucepan over a very low heat. Stir in the lemon juice. Pour the mixture over the breadcrumbs. Roll and cut the left-over pastry into thin strips and make a lattice pattern over the tart. Cook for 25-30 minutes until golden brown. Serve hot or cold with whipped cream. Serves 6.

Rhubarb and Orange Crunchy Crumble

The crumble topping to this stewed rhubarb pudding is distinguished by the use of muesli and wholemeal flour.

1 lb rhubarb, washed, topped and tailed and cut into 1 inch lengths	**CRUMBLE TOPPING**
	4 oz wholemeal flour
	2 oz muesli
2 oz granulated sugar	3 oz butter
1 tablespoon water	2 oz soft brown sugar
Juice of one orange	Grated rind of one orange

Set oven to 350°F or Mark 4. Place the rhubarb, granulated sugar and water into a large saucepan and simmer, uncovered, until the rhubarb is soft. Remove the rhubarb with a draining spoon and place in a deep, ovenproof dish. Reduce the liquid in the saucepan until syrupy and then stir in the orange juice; pour over the rhubarb. For the topping, rub the butter into the flour and stir in the muesli, brown sugar and orange rind. Distribute the crumble mix evenly over the rhubarb and cook in the oven for 30 minutes. Serve hot or cold with plenty of cream. Serves 4.

Bakewell Pudding

This recipe first happened by mistake, when the cook at the Rutland Arms at Bakewell in Derbyshire put the egg mixture on top of the jam instead of on to the pastry for a special strawberry tart.

8 oz puff pastry

FILLING

Strawberry jam	**4 oz butter**
4 egg yolks	**4 oz sugar**
2 egg whites	**Almond essence**

Set over to 425ºF or Mark 7. Roll out the pastry on a lightly floured surface and line a wide, shallow dish or a pie plate and trim. Spread the pastry with a thick layer of strawberry jam. Cream the butter and sugar in a bowl, mix in the egg yolks, the beaten egg whites and the almond essence. Spread this egg mixture over the jam in the dish. Bake for 15 minutes and then reduce heat to 350°F or Mark 4 for 20 minutes. The filling is meant to remain soft and is not intended to set. Serves 4 to 6.

Cherry and Almond Pie

*This cherry flan, with an almond butter filling, comes from the county of Kent
which is famous for its cherry orchards.*

1 lb cherries   1 egg
The weight of the egg in each of the following ingredients:
Butter   Self-raising flour
Caster sugar   Ground almonds

A few drops of almond essence

Set oven to 350°F or Mark 4. Wash and de-stalk the cherries and remove the stones,
if preferred. Grease a shallow ovenproof dish and place the cherries in it. Cream the
butter and the sugar together in a bowl. Beat in the egg, then fold in the flour,
almonds and the almond essence. Spread the mixture evenly over the fruit, put in
the oven and bake for approximately 20-25 minutes or until the mixture is risen and
golden brown. Serve with custard or cream. Serves 2 to 3.

Lemon Chester Pudding

A pudding which dates back to mid-Victorian times and has a tangy lemon filling.

8 oz prepared shortcrust pastry	**4 oz granulated sugar**
2 oz butter	**4 large eggs, separated**
The finely grated rind and the juice of a lemon	**½ oz almonds, very finely chopped**
	3 oz caster sugar

Set oven to 375°F or Mark 5. Roll out the pastry on a lightly floured surface and use to line a well greased 8 inch flan case with a removable base, trimming the edges neatly. Bake blind for 10-15 minutes or until lightly golden. Melt the butter in a saucepan, then remove from the heat and whisk in the lemon rind and juice, the granulated sugar and the egg yolks, continuing to whisk until the mixture is smooth. Stir in the almonds and return to the heat, stirring until hot, but not boiling. Spoon into the pastry case and smooth over; it will be beginning to set. Increase the oven temperature to 425°F or Mark 7. Whisk the egg whites until they stand up in soft peaks, then fold in half the caster sugar. Spoon this mixture over the lemon filling, roughing up to peaks with a fork, then sprinkle on the remainder of the sugar. Bake for 5 minutes, then reduce the temperature to 325°F or Mark 3 and bake for a further 20-30 minutes until the meringue is crisp and a rich golden colour. Serve warm or cold with cream. Serves 4 to 6.

Bachelor's Pudding

A whimsically named farmhouse pudding that was popular in the Victorian era.

2 or 3 cooking apples, peeled,
cored and chopped to provide
4 oz of apple flesh
4 oz fresh white breadcrumbs
4 oz currants or sultanas
3 oz caster sugar
½ teaspoon baking powder

Grated rind of half a lemon
Pinch grated nutmeg
Pinch salt
1 dessertspoon melted butter
2 small eggs, beaten
A little milk

Butter a 2 pint pudding basin. In a bowl, mix together the apples, breadcrumbs, dried fruit and sugar and then stir in the lemon rind, nutmeg and salt. Add the melted butter and the eggs, stir well, cover and leave to stand in a cool place for 20 to 30 minutes. Then mix in sufficient milk to give a dropping consistency and stir in the baking powder. Spoon into the pudding basin and smooth over. Cover with buttered greaseproof paper and seal with kitchen foil. Place in a steamer set over a saucepan of boiling water and steam for 2½-3 hours, topping up the water as necessary. Turn out on to a warm serving plate and serve with custard. Serves 4 to 6.

Pippin Pie

Whole apples baked under a pastry crust.

2 eating apples per person,
preferably pippins
1 orange to every 4 apples
1 piece of cinnamon stick per apple

1 or 2 cloves per apple
Almonds
Sultanas
8 oz shortcrust pastry

Set oven to 375°F or Mark 5. Peel and core the apples and place them in a greased pie dish. Fill the centre of each apple with a few almonds and sultanas and a piece of cinnamon stick. Push the cloves into each apple and sprinkle over the grated rind of the orange(s). Squeeze the orange(s) and pour the juice over the apples. Roll out the pastry on a lightly floured surface and cover the dish, trimming and decorating as preferred. Bake for approximately 35-40 minutes until the apples are cooked and the pastry is brown. Serve with custard or cream. Serves 4.

'In full cry'

Gotham Pudding

A steamed batter pudding with candied peel named after the Nottinghamshire village connected with the tales of 'The Wise Men of Gotham'.

4 eggs, separated	**1 pint milk**
6 oz flour	**4 oz chopped candied or**
Pinch of salt	**mixed peel**
2 oz sugar	**A little extra sugar**

Beat the egg yolks lightly together. Sift the flour and salt into a bowl and stir in the sugar. Make a well in the centre of the flour mixture and add the egg yolks, together with a little milk. Beat until the mixture is completely smooth, then gradually stir in the remainder of the milk. Add the peel. Whisk the egg whites until they stand up in stiff peaks, then fold into the mixture. Turn into a well buttered 1½-2 pint pudding basin, cover with greaseproof paper and seal with kitchen foil. Place in a saucepan with sufficient boiling water to come half-way up the side of the basin and steam for 1-1½ hours, topping up the water when necessary. Turn out the pudding on to a heated serving dish, sprinkle with the extra sugar and serve with cream or custard. Serves 4 to 6.

Marmalade Pudding

A marmalade sponge pudding served with a tangy, marmalade sauce.

3 tablespoons orange marmalade
4 oz self-raising flour
4 oz caster sugar
4 oz soft margarine
1 level teaspoon baking powder
2 medium eggs

Grated rind one orange
SAUCE
4 tablespoons orange marmalade
¼ pint water/orange juice mixed
2 level teaspoons arrowroot
2 tablespoons cold water

Grease a 2 pint pudding basin and place 3 tablespoons marmalade in the base. Put the flour, sugar, margarine, baking powder, eggs and orange rind into a large bowl, mix and beat well for 2-3 minutes until soft and a smooth consistency. Put this sponge mixture on top of the marmalade in the basin. Cover with a circle of greaseproof paper and then seal with kitchen foil. Cover and steam for 2 hours. Prepare the sauce by warming together in a pan the marmalade and water/orange juice and simmer for 5 minutes. Blend the arrowroot and cold water to a smooth cream and stir in some of the marmalade mix. Return to the pan and heat, stirring until the sauce thickens and clears. Turn out the pudding on to a warm plate and serve hot with the sauce. Serves 4 to 6.

Christmas Pudding

This traditional recipe dates from Dickensian times.

8 oz raisins	**5 oz butter**
10 oz currants	**5 large eggs, beaten**
10 oz sultanas	**1 apple, grated**
4 oz mixed peel	**2 oz ground almonds**
16 oz soft brown sugar	**1 orange, grated and squeezed**
2 oz glacé cherries	**2 tablespoons brandy**
8 oz breadcrumbs	**½ teaspoon mixed spice**
8 oz flour	**½ teaspoon ground nutmeg**
5 oz shredded suet	**½ teaspoon almond essence**

½ teaspoon vanilla essence

Chop raisins, quarter glacé cherries and mix all dried fruit together; add grated apple, breadcrumbs, flour, spices, sugar, ground almonds and suet. Melt butter and stir into dry ingredients with orange rind and juice and brandy. Add beaten eggs and almond and vanilla essence. Mix all very thoroughly. Put into greased pudding basins. Cover each basin with greaseproof paper and kitchen foil. Stand in saucepan of boiling water half way up basin and simmer for 7-8 hours, topping up water when necessary. When cooked, renew greaseproof paper and foil. Steam again for 1½-2 hours before serving. Serve with brandy sauce, brandy butter, custard or double cream.

'The holly seller'

Crumbly Fruit Pudding

The addition of ground rice lightens this suet pudding and gives it a crumbly texture.

4 oz self-raising flour	**2 oz soft brown sugar**
2 oz ground rice	**2 oz golden syrup**
4 oz chopped suet	**1 egg**
4 oz mixed dried fruit	**6 tablespoons milk**

Sieve the flour into a mixing bowl and add all the dry ingredients. In a separate bowl warm the golden syrup, beat in the egg and then add the milk and stir. Add the syrup mixture to the dry ingredients and mix to a soft, dropping consistency. Turn the mixture into a greased 1½ pint pudding basin, cover with greaseproof paper and seal with kitchen foil. Steam for 3-3½ hours, topping up the water as necessary, turn out and serve hot, with custard. Serves 4 to 6.

Plum and Apple 'Dumpling'

Not really a dumpling at all, but a steamed plum and apple pudding.

8 oz flour
1 teaspoon baking powder
Pinch of salt
4 oz shredded suet
¼ pint water
1 lb plums, washed and stoned
8 oz cooking apples, peeled
  cored and sliced

6 oz sugar
1 tablespoon stale sponge
  cake crumbs or fresh white
  breadcrumbs
1 tablespoon water to which
  a teaspoon of lemon juice
  has been added
A 'walnut' of butter

Mix the flour, baking powder and salt in a bowl, then stir in the suet. Add the water and mix to a soft dough. Turn out on to a lightly floured surface, knead lightly, then roll out and use to line a buttered 2 pint pudding basin, reserving a portion of the dough for a lid. Fill the basin with alternate layers of plums, apples and sugar, sprinkling the crumbs in between. Add the water and the 'walnut' of butter. Top with the reserved dough, damping the edges and pressing down well to seal. Cover with buttered greaseproof paper and seal with kitchen foil. Steam for 2½-3 hours, topping up the water as necessary. Serve with custard or cream. Serves 4 to 6.

Apple and Oat Betty

An apple pudding layered with a spicy, rolled oats mixture.

3 oz flour	3 oz demerara sugar
3 oz fine rolled oats	2 large cooking apples, peeled
1 teaspoon ground cinnamon	cored and sliced
½ teaspoon mixed spice	Rind and juice of one lemon
4 oz butter	2 tablespoons orange marmalade

Set oven to 375°F or Mark 5. Put the flour, oats and spices into a large bowl. Add 3 oz. of the butter and cut into pieces with a knife and then rub into the dry ingredients until the mixture resembles breadcrumbs. Stir in the sugar. Toss the prepared apples in the lemon juice, rind and marmalade. Grease a 1½-2 pint ovenproof dish. Put half the apples in the dish and sprinkle half the oat mixture over them. Top this with the remaining apples and finally the rest of the oat mixture. Dot the top with the remaining 1 oz butter. Cook for 45 minutes to 1 hour until the apples are tender and the topping is crispy. Serve warm. Serves 4.

Sticky Toffee Pudding

This baked date pudding is topped with a soft caramel toffee sauce.

PUDDING

6 oz stoned dates, roughly chopped	8 oz flour
½ pint boiling water	1 teaspoon baking powder
2 oz butter	1 medium egg
6 oz caster sugar	1 teaspoon bicarbonate of soda
	1 teaspoon vanilla essence

TOFFEE SAUCE

2 oz butter   3 oz soft brown sugar
2 tablespoons double or single cream

Set oven to 350°F or Mark 4. Pour the boiling water over the dates and the bicarbonate of soda and leave to stand. Cream the butter and sugar together in a bowl until pale in colour. Gradually stir in the egg, flour and baking powder. Stir in the dates with the liquid and lastly add the vanilla essence. Put the mixture into a greased 2½ pt ovenproof dish and bake for approximately 40 minutes until risen and firm to the touch. Make the sauce by boiling the ingredients together for 2 minutes and pour over the warm pudding. Serves 4 to 6.

Norfolk Treacle Tart

*This variation of the more usual treacle tart recipe is sometimes called Walpole House
Treacle Tart because of its association with the famous Walpole family of Norfolk.
Originally it was made with black treacle.*

8 oz shortcrust pastry	**½ oz butter, melted**
7 tablespoons golden syrup	**2 tablespoons single cream**
Grated rind and juice of ½ lemon	**2 medium eggs, beaten**

Set oven to 350°F or Mark 4. Grease a 7 inch flan dish. Roll out the pastry on a
lightly floured surface and line the dish and trim. Warm the syrup in a saucepan
until it thins, remove from the heat and then stir in the lemon rind and juice, butter
and cream. Strain the beaten egg into the mixture and combine gently. Pour into the
pastry case and bake for 35-40 minutes or until the filling is set and lightly golden.
Serve hot or cold with cream. Serves 4 to 6.

Chocolate Fudge Pudding

A chocolate sponge pudding with a deliciously sticky chocolate sauce.

PUDDING
4 oz butter
4 oz caster sugar
2 medium eggs
3 oz self-raising flour
2 tablespoons cocoa powder

½ teaspoon vanilla essence
1-2 tablespoons milk
SAUCE
4 oz soft brown sugar
2 tablespoons cocoa powder
½ pint boiling water

Set oven to 375°F or Mark 5. Place all the pudding ingredients into a bowl and beat well to a soft consistency or use a food processor. Put into a 2½ pint ovenproof dish. Make the sauce by combining the sugar and cocoa in a bowl and adding the hot water. Mix well. Pour this sauce over the pudding mixture. Bake for 40 minutes. Turn out the pudding and a thick chocolate sauce will have formed, coating the light sponge pudding. It is delicious served with thick cream. Serves 4 to 6.

Apricot Pudding

*Although this recipe is termed an apricot pudding it is really a
form of apricot pie.*

1 large tin apricots in juice or	**1½ oz sugar**
1½ lbs fresh apricots, poached	**2 eggs, beaten**
2 oz fresh white breadcrumbs	**1 tablespoon white wine (optional)**
¼ pint single cream	**1 teaspoon grated lemon rind**

8 oz shortcrust pastry

Set oven to 350°F or Mark 4. Drain the apricots well and sieve or process through a blender to purée. Place the breadcrumbs in a bowl, heat the cream thoroughly, but do not allow to boil, then stir into the breadcrumbs. Allow to cool, then stir in the sugar, beaten egg, wine if desired and lemon rind. Stir in the apricot purée and turn into a well buttered, 1½ pint shallow pie dish or flan dish. Roll out the pastry on a lightly floured surface and use to cover the apricot filling, trimming it neatly and sealing the edges well. Use the trimmings to decorate and make a small steam hole in the lid. Brush with a little milk or beaten egg to glaze and cook for 30-40 minutes until the pastry is golden. Sprinkle with a little caster sugar and serve hot, with custard or cream. Serves 4.

Syrup and Ginger Roll

A traditional steamed suet roly-poly.

8 oz prepared suet pastry   **1 teaspoon ground ginger**
4 oz golden syrup   **or the grated rind of a lemon**

Roll out the suet pastry on a lightly floured surface to form a strip 8-10 inches long. Spread the syrup to within 1 inch of the edges and sprinkle with the ginger or lemon rind. Roll up the pastry very carefully and seal the edges securely with a little milk or water, to prevent the syrup seeping out. Roll up in a clean, floured pudding cloth and tie the ends, but leave room for the pudding to swell. Steam over a saucepan of boiling water for 1½ hours, topping up the water as necessary. Serve the pudding cut into slices, accompanied by a warm syrup sauce, flavoured with a little ground ginger or with lemon juice. Serves 4 to 6.

METRIC CONVERSIONS

The weights, measures and oven temperatures used in the preceding recipes can be easily converted to their metric equivalents.

Weights

Avoirdupois	Metric
1 oz.	just under 30 grams
4 oz. (¼ lb.)	app. 115 grams
8 oz. (½ lb.)	app. 230 grams
1 lb.	454 grams

Liquid Measures

Imperial	Metric
1 tablespoon (liquid only)	20 millilitres
1 fl. oz.	app. 30 millilitres
1 gill (¼ pt.)	app. 145 millilitres
½ pt.	app. 285 millilitres
1 pt.	app. 570 millilitres
1 qt.	app. 1.140 litres

Oven Temperatures

	°Fahrenheit	Gas Mark	°Celsius
Slow	300	2	140
	325	3	158
Moderate	350	4	177
	375	5	190
	400	6	204
Hot	425	7	214
	450	8	232
	500	9	260

Flour as specified in these recipes refers to Plain Flour unless otherwise described.